KV-702-135

CONTENTS

WHAT IS A NUT?

A nut is the dry fruit or seed of certain plants. It is wrapped with a thin rind and protected by a hard shell. When they are ripe, nuts fall from their plant to the ground. Some will grow into new plants, while others are eaten by animals or people. But people use nuts in lots of other ways, too.

Hard nuts

Nuts grow in lots of different ways. The green shell or husk of a hazelnut hardens and goes brown as it ripens. Acorns grow in the same way.

Soft drupes

The tasty part of a walnut, the kernel, is found inside a hard shell. But the whole nut is found inside a soft, fleshy fruit. This type of nut is called a drupe. Almonds are also drupes.

What is a chestnut?

Horse chestnuts (right) and sweet chestnuts look alike but the trees they come from are completely different. People eat sweet chestnuts but not horse chestnuts. The hard horse chestnut is very good for playing conkers, though!

Both horse chestnuts and sweet chestnuts form inside green cases, which are often prickly. When the nuts are ripe, the cases burst open, scattering the nuts on the ground.

Capsules

These Brazil nuts grow inside a sort of case, or capsule, too. But the Brazil nut capsule is huge! It is also very thick and tough, like wood. Inside, it can contain lots of nuts with very hard, tough shells.

A FEAST OF NUTS

We eat some nuts raw. Others are used in cooking. Farmers grow nuts for us or gather them for their animals. Pigs and squirrels hunt for nuts as well.

Lucky squirrel!
A red squirrel is tackling a prickly chestnut husk. Squirrels make hidden stores of all kinds of nuts. They eat the stores in winter – if they can find them!

A spicy nut
You would not eat a nutmeg whole! These nuts are ground or grated into a powder and used as a spice. They add flavour to many dishes.

Nutmegs grow on evergreen trees in Southern Asia, the West Indies and Brazil. The seed has a thin layer of fleshy fibre around it, which is dried to give mace, the red spice on the right. A tough case (centre) protects the seed.

Harvesting almonds

Can you see the farm worker inside the yellow net? He is harvesting nuts on a huge almond farm in northern Spain. The tree is shaken and the nuts that fall from it are caught in the net. Almonds are grown for their oil as well as for food.

Nutty dishes

Flaked almonds are sprinkled over this lemon flan. Ground almonds and almond paste are just as delicious.

Nuts can be used in sweet and savoury recipes. How many nutty dishes can you think of?

SHINY AND SMOOTH

Most nuts contain rich oil. People crush them up to extract the oil. It's hard to believe that nut oils are used to make hand cream, soap and margarine!

Smooth hands
Rich oils are made from crushing nuts such as almonds and coconuts. Theses are used to make creamy hand and body lotions.

Precious palm oil
Thousands of yellow palm-oil nuts lie outside a mill in Malaysia. The nuts give a strong flavoured oil. It is used to fry foods, and in making margarine and soap. The oil is full of vitamin A, so it is very good for you. The flesh around the nut gives oil, too. It is bright orange.

Nutty butter
This bowl of brown butter has been made from shea nuts in north-west Ghana. Shea nut oil is also used to make margarine and burnt in lamps!

Washing with nuts
These bars of soap in a Nigerian market contain oil taken from the tallow nut. The soap is called black soap because of its unusual colour.

11

NUTS IN A CUP

Nuts can quench your thirst. Some are ground up to make drinks like coffee and cocoa. Others, such as coconuts, are full of a cool and refreshing juice.

A coconut cup

Young coconuts contain a sweet, watery juice. In Oman, in the Middle East, two thirsty travellers sip it through straws.

Hot coffee

In Kenya, bright red coffee berries have been plucked from a bush. The nutty beans inside will be dried, roasted and ground. The powder can be made into a cup of hot coffee.

Another nutty drink
Almonds like these can be made into a sweet milk. They are peeled, pounded and soaked in water. The mixture is then strained and squeezed through muslin.

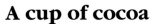

A cup of cocoa
These bright orange beans make delicious hot cocoa. They are harvested from cacao trees in South America. The nuts are then made to ferment, which means they rot slightly and go frothy. After this they are dried, as in the picture. The cocoa kernels inside are then roasted and pressed to make flat cocoa cakes. These are ground into cocoa powder.

NASTY NUTS

Some nuts contain poisonous chemicals that are bad for us, but people still manage to find amazing uses for them all the same.

Catching fish with nuts
In Senegal, fishermen use poison made from nuts to stun fish. The stunned fish float on the water, making them easy to catch. Some of the fish on this stall may have been caught with nuts.

Take care with cashew nuts!

Cashew nuts hang in their green husks from red, fleshy stalks. Roasted cashew nuts are very tasty, as are the red stalks. But the raw shells are poisonous and the whole nut must be roasted to make it safe to eat. In villages on the coast of Kenya, the cashew crop is set alight in a pit. Everyone then sits around the dying fire and removes the cooling husks.

Bright but deadly!

These attractive akee apple nuts contain poisons when they are unripe or over-ripe. The poisons are used to stun fish (see opposite).

NICE NUTS

Some nuts contain chemicals that help us. Many nuts are full of healthy vitamins. Other kinds of nut help to make water safe to drink.

Cleaning the water
In parts of Africa and India, certain nuts are used to clean the water. In Uganda, maringa nuts are used. The nuts attract diseases in the water, which is then filtered.

Healthy nuts
In West Africa, nuts from the locust-bean tree are made into flat black 'cakes'. These contain vitamin B. The yeasty-flavoured cakes are crumbled, like stock cubes, into soups and stews.

A forest of good nuts
The tropical forests of Burma contain the ngapi tree. Its nut seems to help people with an illness called diabetes. The nut is eaten raw or boiled.

17

COCONUTS FOR EVERYONE

Coconuts are grown in tropical countries all around the world. And coconut is eaten and used in cooking just about everywhere.

Green but good
Half-ripe coconuts are just as tasty as ripe ones. The tops are sliced off and the clear, jelly-like flesh scooped out. It is eaten raw or cooked.

Collecting coconuts
In Brazil, a coconut harvester uses a sling around his legs and the palm trunk to help him up. Sometimes, a sling goes round the waist. In Sumatra, people have trained monkeys to harvest coconuts.

Grating coconuts

In Sri Lanka, a coconut is grated using a special knife. In East Africa, cooks sit on a stool with a jagged blade stuck to its front. The coconut is grated around the blade.

Grated coconut is used in spicy food, or fried with sugar. An oil is made by boiling the gratings in water.

Dried coconuts

In Goa, India, coconuts are being dried in the sun. The hard flesh is called copra. It is pressed to give a rich oil, which is used in cooking and margarine.

A SUPER NUT

Coconuts are not just good to eat. People can use them to make soap, oil, rope and even more. For people, a coconut is a super nut!

Coconut rope
Stringy fibre covers coconut husks. In Oman, a woman strips the fibre for rope-making. Coconut rope used to be used on Arab sailing ships.

Hundreds of husks
This heap of coconut husks is lying outside a large factory in Sri Lanka. The fibre, called coir, will be separated from the shell. Coir is used to make rope, cord, matting and furniture stuffing. The hard shell is made into charcoal that burns at very high temperatures.

Chopping up coconuts

In the Seychelle Islands, dried coconuts are being chopped up before making oil from them. The oil is not only used in cooking.

Beautiful coconuts

Coconut oil is made into skin lotion, soap, shampoo, hair oils and conditioners. Many of these things are made in this factory on the island of Tahiti.

Candles are made from the oil, too. And the pressed coconut left over from oil-making is used in fertiliser and animal feed.

Nuts on a String

People use nuts as beads and buttons. Others they can carve into amazing shapes.

Nuts, feathers and beads

This pendant was carved from a nut in New Guinea 200 years ago. It was decorated with coloured beads and a feather on top.

Strings of beads

This Yanomami girl is wearing nuts. She lives in the rainforest of South America. Here, there are hundreds of types of nut to use as beads, like those strung around her neck.

A nut rosary

A Buddhist monk outside a monastery in northern India holds a long string of nut beads. This is called a rosary. The monk will sit quietly by himself and think deeply as he counts the beads one by one. This helps him to concentrate.

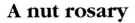

Carving nuts

These ivory nuts are about the size of a hen's egg. They grow on palm trees in Central America. As the nuts ripen, they become hard and creamy-coloured, just like ivory. Buttons, ornaments and even chessmen are carved from them.

23

NUTTY COLOURS

You might not think that nuts can give us bright colours, but they can. People make lots of dyes and inks from nuts.

The red betel nut

This woman from Thailand has been chewing betel nuts. They make her mouth and lips very red. The nut grows on a palm in eastern tropical countries.

Walnut colours

A yellow dye is made by boiling walnut husks. The boiled nuts give a strong brown colour. For hundreds of years, walnut oil has been used to make artists' paints.

Ink from a nut
This ink drawing of marching elephants comes from Thailand. In parts of Asia, a strong, dark ink like this can be made from the rind of the marking nut.

Paint from cones
The nuts of the giant sequoia tree of North America form inside the tree's cones. When the nuts fall from the cones, they can be gathered and made into a deep red paint.

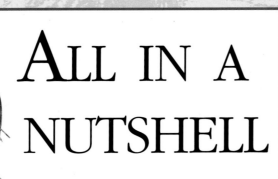

ALL IN A NUTSHELL

Nutshells can be as useful as the nuts they contain. The shells can be made into bowls, ladles and even fertiliser!

Shiny pots

In parts of Africa, oyster nuts grow inside huge gourds. The shells often have lots of stringy fibres which can be used to polish pots.

The fibres round coconut shells are very tough. They are good for scouring out cooking pots. Brushes are made from the fibre, too.

Nutty spoons

Gourd shells grow on vines and contain many nut seeds. Gourds can be made into ladles. Brazil nut capsules and coconut shells make good cups and bowls, too.

Nuts in flowerbeds!

Covering a flowerbed with cocoa shells may seem strange. But cocoa shells help keep the soil moist. They also stop weeds from growing. Cocoa shells are made into fertiliser, too.

Coconut buttons

In this factory in the Seychelle Islands, buttons are made from coconut shells.

Coconut shells can also be ground into flour. This is used as a filler in plastic-making. Crushed shells can be used on flowerbeds like cocoa shells, too.

FIND OUT FOR YOURSELF

See how many things you can make with nuts. Here are some ideas to get you started.

Walnut tortoises

It is easy to make these walnut tortoises:
• Crack a walnut carefully in half. You can eat the insides!
• Mould some Plasticine or modelling clay into the half-shell to make a base.
• Shape the head, legs and tail and push them underneath the shell to attach them on to the base.
You could make beetles and spiders in the same way.

Nutty jewellery

Nuts can be used to decorate badges, brooches and earrings like these. Make the backs for the badges and brooches from card and a safety pin. You can buy earring backs from craft shops. Stick the nuts on their mounts with PVC glue. Paint glue over the nuts as well to make them shiny.

Cooking with nuts

There are thousands of dishes and snacks you can make with nuts. Here are three simple ideas, but you can find lots more in recipe books:

• Crunch almonds and walnuts into small pieces using a rolling pin. Then sprinkle them on breakfast cereal, yoghurt or chocolate mousse.

• On a hot day, take a glass of cold milk, mix in a large spoonful of plain yoghurt and a teaspoon of chopped mint. Then stir in a teaspoon of desiccated (dried) coconut. Very refreshing!

Warning: Some people are allergic to nuts and eating them can make them very ill. Check your friends don't have a nut allergy before giving them nutty food.

• Nuts are tasty in a salad. Grate two large carrots, then mix in a handful of sultanas and some chopped walnuts.

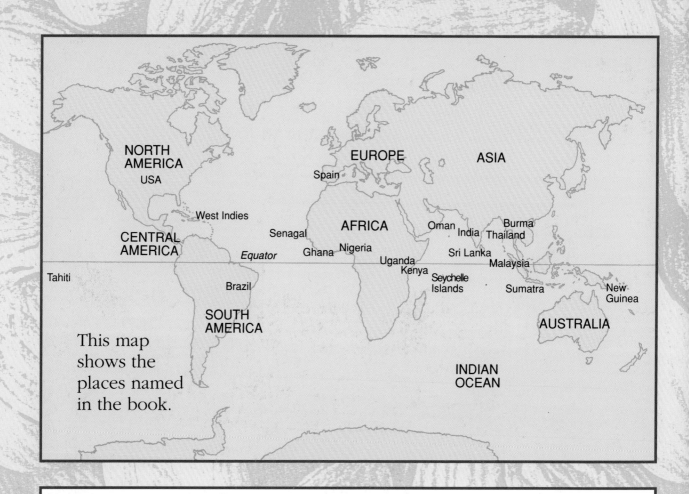

This map shows the places named in the book.

INDEX